~The~
CHRISTMAS
LETTERS
Leader Guide

The Christmas Letters
Celebrating Advent with Those Who Told the Story First

The Christmas Letters
978-1-7910-3323-1
978-1-7910-3325-5 eBook

The Christmas Letters: DVD
978-1-7910-3327-9

The Christmas Letters: Leader Guide
978-1-7910-3324-8
978-1-7910-3326-2 eBook

Also by Magrey R. deVega

Awaiting the Already:
An Advent Journey Through the Gospels

The Bible Year:
A Journey Through Scripture in 365 Days

Embracing the Uncertain:
A Lenten Study for Unsteady Times

Questions Jesus Asked:
A Six-Week Study in the Gospels

Savior:
What the Bible Says about the Cross

With April Casperson, Ingrid McIntyre, and Matt Rawle
Almost Christmas:
A Wesleyan Advent Experience

LEADER GUIDE

Magrey R. deVega

The Christmas Letters

Celebrating Advent
with Those Who Told the Story First

Abingdon Press | Nashville

The Christmas Letters
*Celebrating Advent with Those Who Told the Story First
Leader Guide*

Copyright © 2024 Abingdon Press
All rights reserved.

No part of this work may be reproduced or transmitted in any form or by any means, electronic or mechanical, including photocopying and recording, or by any information storage or retrieval system, except as may be expressly permitted by the 1976 Copyright Act, the 1998 Digital Millennium Copyright Act, or in writing from the publisher. Requests for permission can be addressed to Rights and Permissions, The United Methodist Publishing House, 810 12th Avenue South, Nashville, TN 37203-4704 or emailed to permissions@abingdonpress.com.

978-1-7910-3324-8

Scripture quotations unless otherwise noted are from the Common English Bible. Copyright © 2011 by the Common English Bible. All rights reserved. Used by permission.

Scripture quotation marked NRSVue is taken from the New Revised Standard Version, Updated Edition. Copyright © 2021 National Council of Churches of Christ in the United States of America. Used by permission. All rights reserved worldwide.

MANUFACTURED IN THE UNITED STATES OF AMERICA

CONTENTS

To the Leader 7

Session 1. Good News: 13
    Looking Back to Look Ahead
    (*Romans 1:1-7*)

Session 2. Love Incarnate: 27
    The Word of Life Revealed
    (*1 John 3–4*)

Session 3. Fully Human: 41
    Joy in Humility
    (*Philippians 2:1-11*)

Session 4. Fully Divine: 53
    Peace through Christ
    (*Colossians 1:15-20*)

TO THE LEADER

Many Christians turn to the Gospels of the New Testament or the Prophets of the Old Testament during the Advent season, but fewer turn to the Epistles of the New Testament. Yet the Epistles hold rich resources for those who want to delve further into their spiritual journeys during Advent. As the Epistles reflect on the nature of Christ, consider the nature of Jesus's lordship, and find the incipience of the cross within the Incarnation, as they invite us to enter the Christmas story on a fresh and deep level. Yet few authors have tackled these writings in conjunction with Advent and Christmas themes.

Enter Magrey deVega's *The Christmas Letters*. With the framing of ancient letters from New Testament writers on one hand and the author's composed "letters from God" on the other, *The Christmas Letters* offers readers an intimate journey toward Christmas steeped in the theological richness of our sacred writings. With reflection questions posed throughout the lyrical narrative, *The Christmas Letters* poses a natural opportunity for group conversation and growth. The author writes in the introduction:

> Imagine that, tucked among the piles of Christmas letters from family and friends, there waits for you a stack of correspondence from the greatest sender of all: the God who created you, loves you, and draws near to you in Jesus. Wouldn't those be letters worth cherishing?
>
> This study centers on a special set of letters that were delivered thousands of years ago to the earliest Christian communities in the first-century Greco-Roman world. They were not Christmas letters, but they were letters

Introduction

about Jesus. They were not specifically about his birth, but they give us the earliest glimpses about what the church believed about the Incarnation—the miracle that God became human.

Some of these letters were written just decades after Jesus was on earth, even while the Gospel accounts were still circulating in oral form before they were written down. All of them represent faithful attempts by the early church to understand who Jesus was and what his life meant for humankind. To read them now, in the light of Advent and Christmas, is to read them as a kind of Christmas letter to the modern-day church, catching us up on how our spiritual ancestors were opening up to the wonder and power of Jesus Christ.

This leader guide provides the resources needed to facilitate four sessions of group conversation on *The Christmas Letters*, perfect for the four weeks of Advent. Steps for preparation, opening activities and prayers, video-viewing instructions, discussion questions, and closing activities can be found in sequential order. Within each session, the biblical passage that features in each chapter receives special attention, with questions for individual verses if desired. Feel free to use as much or as little of this material as is helpful to you. In providing this leader guide, the goal is to remove as much work as possible so you can focus on being present to your own group.

Blessings of hope, love, joy, and peace on you and your community during this Advent season.

TIPS FOR LEADING A GROUP SESSION

- Encourage participants to read the week's chapter before coming to that week's session if possible. But do not let lack of reading keep them from coming or participating.

Introduction

The video lessons for each week will cover the main points of each chapter, and the discussion guide is detailed enough that even unprepared participants will be able to follow along.

- Determine what format for your group will work best. Do you want to meet in person and enjoy the fellowship of being in the same space, or will a virtual session increase inclusivity for people who are limited in movement and transportation or have young children at home without childcare?
- You may wish to set a conversation covenant before you begin. What do participants expect out of your conversations? Respectful engagement? Confidentiality? Mindfulness about self-monitoring how much one is talking? Consider what is most important to you and your group and have a brief discussion with group members at your first session.
- Give time after offering a question for people to stop and reflect. Some people will not immediately have an answer, but if allowed to think, will come up with creative responses. Get comfortable with a little bit of silence.
- Use hands-on, creative activities to get the session flowing. Even adults need a little bit of kinetic fun!
- The more confident you are through having prepared, the easier the session will feel to lead.
- Monitor who in the group is talking, and who is not. Feel free to address questions to individuals (if you don't think doing so will embarrass them), or use a talking stick or stone to regulate participation.
- Mix it up! Consider using conversation pairs if big group conversation is going slowly.

Introduction

- Honor the time. Start and end on time (except by agreement of the group).

Adapting for
Virtual Small Group Sessions

Meeting online is a great option for a number of situations. Online meetings are a welcome opportunity for people to converse while seeing one another's faces when circumstances prevent in-person gathering. Online meetings can also expand the "neighborhood" of possible group members because people can log in from just about anywhere in the world. This also gives those who do not have access to transportation or who prefer not to travel at certain times of day the chance to participate.

One popular option is Zoom. This platform is used quite a bit by businesses. If your church has an account, this can be a good medium. Google Meet, Webex, and Microsoft Teams are other good choices. Individuals can obtain free accounts for each of these platforms, but there may be restrictions (for instance, Zoom's free version limits meetings to 40 minutes). Check each platform's website to be sure you are aware of any such restrictions before you sign up.

Video Sharing

For a video-based study, it's important to be able to screen-share your videos so that all participants can view them in your study session. The good news is, whether you have the videos on DVD or streaming files, it is possible to play them in your session.

- All of the videoconferencing platforms mentioned above support screen-sharing videos. Some have specific requirements for assuring that sound will play clearly in

Introduction

  addition to the videos. Follow your videoconferencing platform instructions carefully, and test the video sharing in advance to be sure it works.
- If you wish to screen-share a DVD video, you may need to use a different media player. Some media players will not allow you to share your screen when you play copyright-protected DVDs. VLC is a free media player that is safe and easy to use. To try this software, download at videolan.org/VLC.
- *What about copyright?* DVDs like those you use for group study are meant to be used in a group setting in "real time." That is, whether you meet in person, online, or in a hybrid setting, Abingdon Press encourages use of your DVD or streaming video.
- *What is allowed?* Streaming an Abingdon DVD over Zoom, Teams, or similar platform during a small group session.
- *What is not allowed?* Posting video of a published DVD study to social media or YouTube for later viewing.
- If you have any questions about permissions and copyright, email permissions@abingdonpress.com.
- The streaming subscription platform Amplify Media makes it easy to share streaming videos for groups. When your church has an Amplify subscription, your group members can sign on and have access to the video sessions.
- Visit AmplifyMedia.com to learn more.

Training and Practice

- Choose a platform and practice using it, so you are comfortable with it. Engage in a couple of practice runs with another person.
- Set up a training meeting.

Introduction

- In advance, teach participants how to log in. Tell them that you will send them an invitation via email, and that it will include a link for them to click at the time of the meeting.
- For those who do not have internet service, let them know they may telephone in to the meeting. Provide them the number and let them know that there is usually a unique phone number for each meeting.
- During the training meeting, show them the basic tools available for them to use. They can learn other tools as they feel more confident.

During the Meetings

- **Early invitations.** Send out invitations at least a week in advance. Many meeting platforms enable you to do this through their software.
- **Early log in.** Participants should log in at least ten minutes in advance, to test their audio and their video connections.
- **Talking/not talking.** Instruct participants to keep their microphones muted during the meeting so extraneous noise from their location does not interrupt the meeting. This includes chewing or yawning sounds, which can be embarrassing! When it is time for discussion, participants can unmute themselves. However, ask them to raise their hand or wave when they are ready to share, so you can call on them. Give folks a few minutes to speak up. They may not be used to conversing in web conferences.

SESSION 1

GOOD NEWS

Looking Back to Look Ahead

(Romans 1:1-7)

SESSION 1

GOOD NEWS

Looking Back to Look Ahead

(Romans 1:1-7)

In this text, deVega deftly links the "present" of the Christmas story to the "past" of the prophetic texts that speak longingly of the Messiah's coming. Hope, though long delayed, cannot ultimately be denied. Jesus, coming himself from a position of exile and disenfranchisement, invites us to walk from our own pain and fear into a life of hope. His long-awaited birth speaks new life into a people living in the shadow of death.

Take care in this session to set a warm, inviting tone for the rest of the study. You may have to invest extra effort in this session to get conversation going, but hopefully, by the end of the session, the group will be engaged in the study with a momentum to carry through the remaining three weeks.

PLANNING THE SESSION

Session Goals

By the end of this session, participants will:

- understand the importance of prophetic texts to the season of Advent,
- consider how the season of Advent leads us to have hope even under difficult circumstances, and
- explore how the historical events surrounding the prophets' writings and New Testament times inform the spiritual significance of their work.

Preparation

- Gather materials needed:
    ◊ Advent wreath with candles
    ◊ Matches or lighter
    ◊ Note cards
    ◊ Slips of paper with the messianic prophecies from the chapter printed on them
    ◊ Writing implements
    ◊ Wrapped gifts centerpiece*
- Read through the chapter and leader guide, and watch the video.
- Pray for the session and its participants.

*You might consider, as a centerpiece for the group, including four wrapped gifts, each one symbolizing the epistle that the respective chapters feature. You could write the name, chapter, and verses of the epistle on the gift tag, and maybe, if you wish to have a participant unwrap a gift each time, include the corresponding virtue on a notecard or a symbolic item within the box:

Gift Tag	Gift	Possible symbolic item
Romans 1:1-7	Hope	Candle
1 John 3–4	Love	Heart-shaped item
Philippians 2:1-11	Joy	Christmas bell
Colossians 1:15-20	Peace	Dove ornament or olive branch

You might consider unwrapping these boxes at the end of each session. Leave the symbolic item as a centerpiece display.

OPENING ACTIVITY AND PRAYER

In the chapter, the author mentions that the year's review is often typical for people in December. Open your session by reading these words aloud from the first chapter of *The Christmas Letters*:

> Grace to you and peace from God our Father and the Lord Jesus Christ. Because Advent is the beginning of the Christian liturgical year, it is appropriate to spend time reflecting on the past year. It begins in the wake of Thanksgiving, when we gather with family and friends to take an inventory of the blessings we have experienced. It ends on the brink of a new calendar year, as we ponder the highs and lows of the past twelve months in anticipation of what lies ahead. Advent prompts us to consider how we have experienced God in the past, and what we long for in the future.

Invite participants to write down a few major events of the past year on note cards. If they are comfortable, invite participants to share one or more significant events from the last year.

Discuss:

- How does recalling the past year influence your hopes and expectations for the year ahead?
- What do you hope for this Advent season?

You will use these cards again in your closing liturgy at the end of the session.

Light the candle of hope on the Advent wreath.

Opening Prayer

God of hope, God of all our days, we come together today, each bearing a year of events, good and difficult. As we share this time together, may your Word clarify both our past and future. Lead us into hope. Amen.

WATCH THE VIDEO

Play session 1: "Good News: Looking Back to Look Ahead" on *The Christmas Letters* DVD or via Amplify Media.

Discuss:

- Did anything specific stand out as you watched the video?
- Magrey deVega describes Advent as "waiting for something that has already happened." When you think about Advent, do you think more about what already happened, or what still is ahead in the future? What is the relationship between the two?
- What do you hope to gain from a study of some of the epistles during Advent?
- What is something you learned in the video that you didn't know before?

Invite the group to keep both the video and the book in mind throughout the discussion below.

STUDY AND DISCUSSION

Before diving into the chapter itself, take time to gain a more thorough understanding of Romans 1:1-7, which is the focus of the author's chapter.

Good News

Read Romans 1:1-7 together, out loud, by assigning different verses to different people. (It is okay if your group uses multiple translations.) Inviting group participants to take turns reading allows you to hear the passage in a variety of voices.

After reading through once, use the questions below to engage with the Scripture in depth. Questions are listed by Bible verse.

¹Paul, a slave of Christ Jesus, called to be an apostle and set apart for God's good news.

- What other "slaves" do we hear of in the Christmas story?
- What background about the word *apostle* do we know?
- Why is Paul "set apart"? Is there something about the Gospel that sets believers apart? What is this "good news," according to Paul?

²God promised this good news about his Son ahead of time through his prophets in the holy scriptures.

- Which promises of the prophets is Paul referring to? Are there specific verses that you understand as referring to Jesus?
- Why does Paul set up his letter beginning with referencing the prophets?
- How do you grapple with the fact that, in the Hebrew Scriptures, the prophecies to which Paul refers had their own historical contexts? For example, the famous verse of Isaiah 7:14 (the "young woman is pregnant and is about to give birth to a son") referred originally to the king Hezekiah, who was instrumental in delivering Jerusalem from the Assyrian king Sennacherib. Typically, however, Christians, including early Christians, have interpreted these Scriptures as referring to Jesus.

- How, as Christians, do we read the Hebrew prophecies respectfully of their original contexts, while also recognizing their pertinence to the life of Jesus?

³His Son was descended from David.

- Refer to the genealogies of Jesus, given in Matthew and Luke. Why is David's lineage so important? What significance does reference to history give Paul?
- The NRSVue translates this verse as "...who was descended from David according to the flesh." Reflect on the use of "flesh" here. How do the Gospels talk about "flesh"? For example, John states that "the Word became flesh" (John 1:14). Is "flesh" necessarily a good or bad thing? How does "flesh" relate to "spirit"?

⁴He was publicly identified as God's Son with power through his resurrection from the dead, which was based on the Spirit of holiness.

- This verse of Romans takes us all the way from Jesus's birth, in verse 3, to his resurrection, in verse 4. What establishes Jesus as the son of God in Romans? Is this consistent with the Gospels' portrayal of events? Or is Paul's representation unique?
- The title of Jesus that Paul emphasizes in this passage is "God's Son." Why do you think he uses this title? What does it convey to you?

⁵Through him we have received God's grace and our appointment to be apostles. This was to bring all Gentiles to faithful obedience for his name's sake.

- "Faithful obedience" might be a confusing phrase. What does it mean to you? Why might it be important? What does "faithful obedience" look like to you?

- Paul has a strong emphasis on bringing the message of the gospel to the Gentiles. Why was this significant?

⁶You who are called by Jesus Christ are also included among these Gentiles.

- The surprise comes at the end of this verse, that the audience themselves are among those whom Paul most wants to reach with his message! How do you think receivers of this letter would respond to the news that Paul had this goal of "faithful obedience" for them?
- Our calling, Paul says, is to be "included" (CEB) or "to belong" (NRSVue). What does inclusion look like to you? What hopes for belonging to Jesus might we have this season of Advent and Christmas?

⁷To those in Rome who are dearly loved by God and called to be God's people.

Grace to you and peace from God our Father and the Lord Jesus Christ.

- This letter is addressed to a specific audience of Romans. Given this specific audience, how do we extend the letter to ourselves, as contemporary Christians?
- What does it mean to be "called to be God's people"? Is this a calling we also share?
- How does it feel to receive a greeting of "grace and peace"? How would it feel to extend this greeting to others you may encounter?

Consider taking some time as well to read messianic prophecies of the Hebrew Bible for an even richer understanding of the scriptural references to Advent. These messianic prophecies reflect a cultural context filled with longing for a hope not yet realized.

Read aloud the following quotation from *The Christmas Letters*:

> To understand the meaning and purpose of the Incarnation, we need to begin by looking at the testimony of the Hebrew prophets. It is no surprise that in the Christian lectionary—the ecumenical reference guide of Sunday Scripture texts for worship—the first Sunday of Advent always points us to prophetic texts. The Old Testament readings are from Isaiah or Jeremiah, and the Gospel readings are prophetic in nature, about interpreting the signs of the inbreaking of God into the world.
>
> Paul quotes or paraphrases the prophets over twenty times in Romans, including references to Habakkuk, Malachi, Hosea, and Jeremiah. By far, Paul cites the words of Isaiah, referencing him nineteen times in his Letter to the Romans.

If you have time, break your large group up into pairs, triplets, and so on and assign one or two of the passages below to each pair or group. Ask each pair or group to look up the passage(s) from Isaiah and explore the following questions. If you would like to, you can have the verses preprinted on index cards to easily distribute them to the groups.

- What is the problem that is being responded to (if there are enough clues from the context to be able to tell)?
- What is being hoped for?
- How are the people's hopes to be fulfilled through the prophecy?
- In what ways does Jesus's life echo this prophecy?

Scripture Passages

- Isaiah 2:4
- Isaiah 11:1, 5-6
- Isaiah 7:14
- Isaiah 64:1-2
- Isaiah 40:1-5
- Isaiah 61:1-2a

You can have each small group report back briefly (1–2 minutes or less). After fully exploring the Scriptures, you can transition to discussing the chapter and relating it more fully to lived experiences of group members.

Now enter into discussion using concepts and questions from the book more specifically.

The Advent season meets us where we are, even when we are struggling to feel the merriment of the season. Yet the prophets, explored in small groups above, have similar feelings of difficulty. Consider the following quotation and questions that the author poses.

> Isaiah inspired a prophetic tradition that went beyond the prophet's life, carrying his message forward to later times and circumstances. The book that bears Isaiah's name warned Judah of the coming destruction by the Babylonian Empire. While Judah was in exile, Isaiah gave them words of hope, encouraging them to maintain their commitment to God, who would bring them a deliverer and return them to their land.

- In what way are you feeling a sense of exile today? How are you longing for "home" in some way?
- How do these Scriptures from Isaiah give you comfort and encouragement?

- How do these Scriptures heighten your anticipation for Jesus Christ?

Nobody comes to their beliefs or spirituality in a vacuum. Just like us, the biblical writers were deeply influenced by their own contexts as they wrote. Magrey deVega writes,

> Jesus was also born into a world of significant political and sociological upheaval....
>
> The arrival of Greco-Roman culture introduced the evolution of new styles of cities, roads, and commerce. Greek and Aramaic became the dominant languages, and Greek philosophers gave rise to new ways of thinking and seeing the world.
>
> The Hebrew people would no longer be called Israelites, as they often were throughout the Old Testament, but Jews, a derivative of Judeans, the Southern Kingdom that had returned from exile now living in the land. They had a temple, and they were living in the land of their ancestors, but they had no political king, no true sense of self-governance and independence.
>
> This was the world into which Jesus was born, and the result was that it gave him a unique language to speak (Aramaic) to a people with a unique mindset (longing for liberation) in a unique geopolitical context (Roman occupation). Everything Jesus would say and do was rooted in the time and place into which he entered the world.
>
> His ministry would be based on a message of hope and deliverance from the powers that oppress us, in a language people could understand. In other words,

he was born just at the right time for this message to endure, for thousands of years, even until today.

Consider how time and place shape the sacred stories we tell as your group discusses these questions from *The Christmas Letters*:

- How did the community you grew up in shape your view of the world?
- How might things be different for you today if you were born in a different time and place?
- How does the fact that Jesus was born in a specific time and place in history give you a deeper understanding of his message for us today?

Confession, rather than blaming or shaming us, draws us more deeply into the mystery of God's grace. Through confession, we experience the mystery of God's mercy. Magrey deVega writes,

> Confession, repentance, and openness to God's forgiveness may seem like an odd invitation during the Advent season. We may more readily associate these activities with Lent and the journey toward the cross. But for Paul and his Letter to the Romans, for the prophets who uttered both words of comfort and challenge to the exiles, and in the name of Jesus who was born in a precise inflection point in history, we are called to surrender ourselves to God.

Consider how repentance and confession can become part of your Advent observance.

- When did making a confession to God or someone else gave you a sense of freedom and release from your mistakes?

- In what way do you need Jesus to be your "Second Adam," helping you to overcome some sin in your life?
- How will you practice confession and repentance at the start of your Advent journey?

Closing Activity and Prayer

Unwrap the appropriate box from the centerpiece and put the item symbolizing hope on display.

Create a litany using the life events participants noted in the opening activities, using the events they wrote on their index cards.

Leader: God of hope, we thank you for this time together, and for the wisdom and light you have cast on our path through our conversation. Knowing that you hold all things in your outstretched hands, we offer you these events of our lives.

[A participant or the group leader shares a life event noted on an index card.]

Group: God of us, you bear witness, and you offer hope.

[A second participant shares a life event noted on an index card.]

Group: God of us, you bear witness, and you offer hope.

[This continues until all who feel comfortable sharing have done so.]

Closing Prayer

You have heard the cries of our hearts, God, and you respond in love. Fulfill our longings and deepen our joy. Lead us into hope as we go out from this place. In Jesus's name. Amen.

SESSION 2

LOVE INCARNATE

The Word of Life Revealed

(1 John 3–4)

SESSION 2

LOVE INCARNATE

The Word of Life Revealed

(1 John 3–4)

Love incarnate enters the world through a newborn baby boy, and the world is forever changed. Our own love toward one another and toward God's world continues the work of God from the Incarnation. As familiar as the first chapter of the Gospel of John is for its hymn celebrating the birth of Jesus through poetic rather than narrative means, the epistle of 1 John will offer group participants a fresh perspective on the theme of love and its centrality to the Advent and Christmas seasons.

PLANNING THE SESSION

Session Goals

By the end of this session, participants will:

- understand what type of love God makes incarnate in the world through Jesus's birth,
- articulate how the "way of truth" and "way of love" coincide in the life and teachings of Jesus,
- connect the great beginnings of Creation in Genesis 1 to the great event of the Incarnation in John 1, and
- consider what types of offerings of love they can make this Advent season.

Preparation

- Gather materials needed
  - ◊ Advent wreath with candles
  - ◊ Matches or lighter
  - ◊ Wrapped gifts centerpiece (see Preparation in session 1)
- Read through the chapter, and leader guide, and watch the video.
- Pray for the session and its participants.

OPENING ACTIVITY AND PRAYER

Author Magrey deVega begins this chapter with a reminder of the central truth of Christianity: God loves us. Open your session by reading aloud this quotation from chapter 2 of *The Christmas Letters*:

> When times are tough, when stressors feel too great to bear, and when decisions seem too difficult to make, we can easily lose sight of the most important truth in our lives.

Invite the group to keep both the video and the book in mind throughout the discussion below.

STUDY AND DISCUSSION

The author uses 1 John 2–3 as his main text in this chapter. Like the Gospel of John, the epistle of 1 John focuses heavily on love. Human love is to emulate God's love, as God is the source of love. Read through the passages selected from 1 John 2–3 together as a group (yes, it's long, but regard it as a conversation between yourself and the Johannine author). Discussion questions are included between large blocks of text, so you can have the opportunity for further dialogue if you would like.

After reading, use the questions below to engage in deeper study of the Scripture passage. Questions are listed after each set of Bible verses.

> *2:1 My little children, I'm writing these things to you so that you don't sin. But if you do sin, we have an advocate with the Father, Jesus Christ the righteous one. ²He is God's way of dealing with our sins, not only ours but the sins of the whole world.*

- What does the word *advocate* bring up for you? Is the image personal, legal, or relational?
- Even though the emphasis on these chapters is love, the idea of sin comes up very quickly. How, in your understanding, do "love" and "sin" exist in such close succession? How does love respond to sin?
- Here, Jesus is called "God's way of dealing with our sins." The NRSVue uses the wording "the atoning sacrifice for our sins." What does this mean to you? For some people, the image of Jesus as sacrifice is difficult or disturbing. How do you respond to it?

God loves us.

And it's not just that God loves *us*. God loves *me*. Just like God loves you. God loves you personally, directly, and closely. It's not just *believing* or *understanding* God's love for you. It is experiencing that love in the deepest part of your being. It is recognizing that the very reason for your existence, and the very fiber of your being, is connected to the love that God has for you. Nothing is more important than that. Nothing else matters more than that.

Invite participants to reflect on and answer the question briefly:

- "What (or whom) do you love? What or whom is on your heart today?"

Light the first two Advent candles.

Opening Prayer

God of love, during this time, open us to the possibility of koinonia, of open-hearted community, with one another. Shine light in the dark places of our hearts, so we can move toward the brightness of your Son. Amen.

WATCH THE VIDEO

Play session 2: "Love Incarnate: The Word of Life Revealed" on *The Christmas Letters DVD* or via Amplify Media.

Discuss:

- Did anything specific stand out as you watched the video?
- What does 1 John teach us about the love we are called to have for one another?
- How would you describe the power of love in our world?
- What is something you learned that you didn't know before?

³This is how we know that we know him: if we keep his commandments. ⁴The one who claims, "I know him," while not keeping his commandments, is a liar, and the truth is not in this person. ⁵But the love of God is truly perfected in whoever keeps his word. This is how we know we are in him. ⁶The one who claims to remain in him ought to live in the same way as he lived.

- These verses talk a lot about "commandments." What commandments, do you suppose, the writer is referring to? The entire Hebrew Torah? The command, given by Jesus as the Greatest Commandment in Matthew 22, to love God and neighbor? Something else?
- The idea of "law" is often very negative for Christians. Is this bad reputation of the law warranted? How do you approach the idea of law?
- Obedience to God's commandments is the purest sign for this biblical writer that someone is in obedience to the law. Do you agree or push back? Why?

⁷Dear friends, I'm not writing a new commandment to you, but an old commandment that you had from the beginning. The old commandment is the message you heard. ⁸On the other hand, I am writing a new commandment to you, which is true in him and in you, because the darkness is passing away and the true light already shines. ⁹The one who claims to be in the light while hating a brother or sister is in the darkness even now. ¹⁰The person loving a brother and sister stays in the light, and there is nothing in the light that causes a person to stumble. ¹¹But the person who hates a brother or sister is in the darkness and lives in the darkness, and doesn't know where to go because the darkness blinds the eyes.

- The writer claims that he is "not writing a new commandment" in verse 7, but in verse 8, states that he "is writing a new commandment." How do you make sense

of this confusion? What is the old commandment, do you suppose, that is heard "from the beginning"?
- What do you suppose gives the author hope that "the darkness is passing away and the true light already shines"?
- Many of us have difficult relationships with family members or community members, both of whom would be covered under the language of "brothers or sisters" in this passage. Some of us have even had to move on from broken relationships for our own health. How do we understand this passage in light of those difficult relationships?

15 Don't love the world or the things in the world. If anyone loves the world, the love of the Father is not in them. 16 Everything that is in the world—the craving for whatever the body feels, the craving for whatever the eyes see and the arrogant pride in one's possessions— is not of the Father but is of the world. 17 And the world and its cravings are passing away, but the person who does the will of God remains forever.

- The overriding emphasis of this book is love—and yet, this passage tells us not to love the things of this world. What do you make of that?

3:1 See what kind of love the Father has given to us in that we should be called God's children, and that is what we are! Because the world didn't recognize him, it doesn't recognize us.

2 Dear friends, now we are God's children, and it hasn't yet appeared what we will be. We know that when he appears we will be like him because we'll see him as he is. 3 And all who have this hope in him purify themselves even as he is pure.

- This writer draws a strong distinction between "the world" and "God's children." What do you think about this distinction? How can we live in the world as God's children?

¹¹*This is the message that you heard from the beginning: love each other.* ¹²*Don't behave like Cain, who belonged to the evil one and murdered his brother. And why did he kill him? He killed him because his own works were evil, but the works of his brother were righteous.*

¹³*Don't be surprised, brothers and sisters, if the world hates you.* ¹⁴*We know that we have transferred from death to life, because we love the brothers and sisters. The person who does not love remains in death.* ¹⁵*Everyone who hates a brother or sister is a murderer, and you know that murderers don't have eternal life residing in them.* ¹⁶*This is how we know love: Jesus laid down his life for us, and we ought to lay down our lives for our brothers and sisters.* ¹⁷*But if someone has material possessions and sees a brother or sister in need but refuses to help—how can the love of God dwell in a person like that?*

- As we know from reading this chapter from *The Christmas Letters*, the writers of the Johannine Epistles make frequent reference to Genesis. Here, there's yet another Genesis reference, very explicitly! How does the reason that Cain murdered Abel give light to our own motives for hatred?
- Laying down one's life for a brother or sister, the writer tells us, is how we know ourselves what love is, and how, in turn, we live out the example of Jesus. How do we know when we are laying down our lives for one another? Is there a way to do this without getting a martyr complex? And if so, what does that look like to you?

¹⁸*Little children, let's not love with words or speech but with action and truth.* ¹⁹*This is how we will know that we belong to the truth and reassure our hearts in God's presence.* ²⁰*Even if our hearts condemn*

us, God is greater than our hearts and knows all things. ²¹*Dear friends, if our hearts don't condemn us, we have confidence in relationship to God.* ²²*We receive whatever we ask from him because we keep his commandments and do what pleases him.*

- Love and action, the writer tells us, go together. How do we love not just in word, but in action?
- What authority do our own hearts have in telling us where we stand before God?

²³*This is his commandment, that we believe in the name of his Son, Jesus Christ, and love each other as he commanded us.* ²⁴*Those who keep his commandments dwell in God and God dwells in them. This is how we know that he dwells in us, because of the Spirit he has given us.*

- What does abiding in God's love look like for you?

Now, turn to a discussion of the book more specifically.

Invite the group to skim over the section titled "1 John, John 1, and Genesis" (pages 38–45 of *The Christmas Letters*). In this section, the author illustrates the close connection between Genesis 1 and John 1, while also exploring how an encounter in a monastery focused his own reflection on the question, "Do you believe that God loves you?" Read aloud this quotation from Magrey deVega:

> Together, these ideas from John 1 and 1 John converge to underscore the most important conviction in the Christian faith: God loves you.
>
> The great God and powerful Creator of the universe, who is the source of all light and life, has not only conquered sin and darkness in the world, but has drawn near to you in Jesus. In the incarnation of Jesus, you have the most tangible expression of God's love, made real for you.

> When Father Ambrose asked me that question that day on my spiritual retreat, about whether I believed that God loved me, I knew that the best and only response I could have in that moment was to remember Jesus. Jesus came to earth "by water and blood," to be a human just like me. He taught the way of love, so that I could be free of my sins, fears, and griefs. He gave up his life in an act of self-giving love, so that I could be in a full relationship with God. And he rose again so that I could be raised to a new way of loving God and loving all people.
>
> So any time I need a reminder of how much God loves me, I just need to think about the birth, life, death, and resurrection of Jesus. So can you.

Magrey's words show us that God's love for us is both cosmic and personal. Consider these reflection questions written by the author:

- How does thinking about the first chapter of Genesis during Advent strengthen your appreciation of the incarnation of Jesus?
- In what ways are you experiencing a darkness in your life that can be overcome by the light of Jesus?
- How would you answer Father Ambrose's question: "Do you believe that God loves you?"
- What difference does your belief make in your life?

The author discusses the delicate balance of truth and love, and how many of us navigate the reality that we can be more like Pharisees, while professing to be Christ followers (see his discussion of the Barna survey in this chapter).

Read aloud this quotation:

> Consider a strained relationship you have had at some point in your life with someone you love. In order for any

loving relationship to work, whether it be in a marriage or a family relationship or a close friendship, there needs to be a balance between speaking and hearing truth, and doing so with love. In a relationship, sometimes the most loving thing you can do is to speak truth to someone, along with being open to hearing hard truths about yourself. And sometimes, the most truthful thing to do is to love that person, even when it's hard.

Consider these questions from the author:

- Why do you think truthfulness is an important aspect of our relationships with one another?
- Why do you think 1 John connects truthfulness with following God's commandments?
- Where do you find yourself among the results and conclusions of the Barna survey?

Putting everything together, the author shows us how practicing the love of God as revealed in Christ brings us into fellowship (the Greek *koinonia*) with one another. Here is the definition of *koinonia* Magrey deVega offers:

> *Koinonia*...has a range of translations in English. Most often, it is translated as *fellowship*, as it is in this verse. It can also be translated as *sharing*, *participation*, and *contribution*. In other words, a community of Christians in fellowship with one another is, in its essence, an active participation, in which people freely give and receive acts of generosity and love with one another.

- When and where have you experienced *koinonia* as the author defines it here?
- Is your congregation a source of *koinonia* for you? For others? What would help you as a church more fully embody this kind of fellowship?

- How will your belief in God's love for you change your perspective and behavior for the better?
- What, in your experience, is the relationship between love and time?
- How will you practice the concepts of showing versus telling, staying connected, and holding your truth lovingly?

CLOSING ACTIVITY AND PRAYER

Unwrap the appropriate box from the centerpiece and put the item symbolizing love on display.

Go around the circle. Invite each participant to name how they will share truth and love in the coming week. Is there a practice, commitment, or discipline they can try to renew energy to love?

Offer these things to God in prayer. Have every participant pray for the offering of truth and love of the person on their right.

Closing Prayer

God of love, you hold all things together. Bind our hearts and minds in harmony as we go out this week, seeking to share your truth and love with the world. For all the intentions named here, and those left unnamed, we invite you to complete and fulfill all that we will leave undone. In the name of Jesus, the light of the world. Amen.

SESSION 3

FULLY HUMAN

Joy in Humility

(Philippians 2:1-11)

Fully
Human

SESSION 3

FULLY HUMAN

Joy in Humility

(Philippians 2:1-11)

    Centering a beloved biblical passage, the Christ hymn of Philippians 2, this chapter of *The Christmas Letters* will inspire group participants to pursue Christlikeness through their own service during this Advent season. Paired with the Philippians passage is a focus on the story of Mary's courageous journey to becoming Jesus's mother, and how her decision to say yes to bearing God in the world carried her from fear into joy.

    Consider, as you prepare for your group this week, what fear or hesitancy you may have, even within your own leadership. Are there areas of reluctance where a "yes" may empower you to lead more joyfully? How can you walk in the footsteps of Mary this week?

PLANNING THE SESSION

Session Goals

By the end of the end of this session, participants will:

- articulate how empathy, curiosity, and humility are part of Paul's message in Philippians;

- understand how Mary is an example of the virtues that Paul discusses; and
- begin to move from fear to joy.

Preparation

- Gather materials needed
  ◊ Advent wreath with candles
  ◊ Matches or lighter
  ◊ Wrapped gifts centerpiece (see Preparation in session 1)
- Read through the chapter and leader guide and watch the video.
- Pray for the session and its participants.

OPENING ACTIVITY AND PRAYER

Paul's Letter to the Philippians points to the union between divinity and humanity. Open your session by reading aloud this quotation from chapter 3 of *The Christmas Letters*:

> In every major scene in the story of Jesus's birth, there is an interaction between the human and the divine. Think about it. Every time we are introduced to a new character in the birth narratives, it is in the context of some divine visitation of an unsuspecting human being....
>
> And what is the common denominator among all these people, all these interactions? They all point to Jesus, who is not just the pivotal character for each of these people, but the bridge between the human and the divine for all the world, for all eternity.
>
> Here is what we know about ourselves as humans, and about our sinful condition: we cannot save ourselves. We need someone who is *more than* human to become

human in order to meet us where we are and to help us become all that God has called us to be.

In short, we need Jesus, who is the bridge between heaven and earth, who, though being God, became human, just like us.

Philippians helps us see that the arrival of Jesus, divine and human, is a source of joy. Elsewhere in the letter Paul writes, "Be glad in the Lord always! Again I say, be glad!" (Philippians 4:4).

Invite participants to name joys as signs of God's presence in their lives.

- What has brought them joy in the past week?
  What joyful things do they look forward to in the coming days and weeks?
- What joy do they find in the celebration of Christ's coming?

Light the first three Advent candles.

Opening Prayer

God, bringer of joy, whatever we are carrying today, let this space be one in which we feel your love warming our souls. Through our time together, let our joy in you multiply. Amen.

WATCH THE VIDEO

Play session 3: "Fully Human: Joy in Humility" on *The Christmas Letters* DVD or via Amplify Media.

Discuss:

- Did anything specific stand out as you watched the video?
- Why do you think Philippians is called the epistle of joy?

- What is the relationship between joy and humility?
- Magrey deVega mentioned four practical aspects of humility. Which of those most resonated with you?
- What is something you learned that you didn't know before?

Invite the group to keep both the video and the book in mind throughout the discussion below.

STUDY AND DISCUSSION

Read through the featured Bible passage of chapter 3 of *The Christmas Letters*, Philippians 2:1-11. Ask group participants to take turns reading so the group can experience different voices delivering the message of Scripture. It is okay if there are multiple translations.

After your group has read through the passage once, use the questions below to study the Scripture passage in depth. Questions are listed after the Bible verses.

> *¹1If there is any encouragement in Christ, any comfort in love, any sharing in the Spirit, any sympathy, ²complete my joy by thinking the same way, having the same love, being united, and agreeing with each other. ³Don't do anything for selfish purposes, but with humility think of others as better than yourselves. ⁴Instead of each person watching out for their own good, watch out for what is better for others.*

- What does Paul say will complete his joy?
- What does the phrase "thinking the same way" mean to you? How does the rest of this section of the text help to illustrate what Paul means?
- What attitudes or actions does Paul advocate in these verses? What does he want his audience to avoid?
- What happens if we disagree, over either trifling or significant matters?

⁵*Adopt the attitude that was in Christ Jesus:*

⁶*Though he was in the form of God,*
he did not consider being equal with God
something to exploit.

- Another translation possibility for the word *though* is *because*. How would reading *because* here change the connotation of the verse?
- Why would being God cause Jesus to empty himself? How do you understand this paradox?
- What is Jesus's relationship to God's power?
- How does Jesus's relationship to power compare with other forms of power that we see around us?

⁷*But he emptied himself*
by taking the form of a slave
and by becoming like human beings.
⁸*When he found himself in in the form of a human,*
he humbled himself by becoming obedient to the point of death,
even death on a cross.

- The word *doulos* in Greek, translated here as "slave," is a strong one. It implies total servitude. While some translations lighten the meaning to "servant," this rendering doesn't capture the full meaning of the term.
- What significance does it carry that Jesus took the form of a slave?
- To what did Jesus become a slave?
- Here, Jesus is said to be "in the form of" a human. Is this the same meaning as incarnation? Why or why not?
- Jesus's obedience leads him to the cross. Is this a path one that everyday humans are meant to follow?

> ⁹*Therefore, God highly honored him*
> > *and gave him a name above all names,*
> > ¹⁰*so that at the name of Jesus everyone*
> > > *in heaven, on earth, and under the earth might bow*
> > > ¹¹*and every tongue confess*
> > > > *that Jesus Christ is Lord, to the glory of God the Father.*

- It seems that God values Jesus's humility more than earthly power, to the extent that God enthrones Jesus above all others. What does this suggest about the distribution of power in God's kingdom?
- Who, ultimately, will worship God as revealed in Jesus? For whom, then, is the gospel teaching?
- Philippians is sometimes called the "joy epistle." Joy is also one of the themes of Advent. How do you see Philippians tying into the story of Christmas, recognizing that Jesus's birth is represented differently in the Gospels?

Now, transition to a discussion of the book material.

The author discusses how, without the intervention of God in Christ, we are all like "misfit toys," out of place, broken, unwanted. Magrey deVega writes,

> Oh, I know, we don't want to admit it. We spend a lot of time and effort trying to project to other people that things are a lot better than they actually are. But you and I well know deep down inside that we have our own hang-ups, habits, and heartaches. We live in relationships that are broken, a past that is full of shame and guilt, and a future that is fraught with worry. We have the constant replay of old tapes in our minds that would convince us that we are far removed from the kind of life we know we should live.

This is a difficult experience that is sadly common for humans.

> If only someone could come and rewrite the script for us. To add a scene. To do for us what we cannot do for ourselves: to come down to earth, join us at our level, maybe even become a misfit toy too, and show us what unconditional love and second chances might look like.

After reading these two quotations aloud, discuss the following questions.

- In what ways do you feel like a "misfit toy"? How do others you know feel like they are "misfit toys"?
- How does the second chapter of Philippians bring you comfort and encouragement?
- How do you think the incarnation of Jesus gives you hope for your situation?

The Christ hymn in Philippians 2 begins with the word *though*: "Though he was in the form of God." Magrey deVega shows, however, that this word can also be translated as *because*: "Because he was in the form of God."

Reading it this way casts new light on the hymn. It means that Jesus didn't overcome the form of God in emptying himself, but rather expressed the form of God by emptying himself. Magrey deVega writes,

> *Because* Jesus was God, he did not consider being God as something to be exploited.
>
> It means there is no contradiction between being God and being self-giving. It suggests that it is within God's very nature to be gracious and generous. The work of Jesus is not God concealed, but God revealed.

In other words, Philippians shows how Jesus behaves in self-giving ways because he is God, not in spite of being God. These qualities are also applicable to normal people.

- How does God's generosity and self-giving shape your understanding of who God is?
- Do you think *because* or *though* is a better translation of this word in Philippians 2:5? Why?
- Of the three qualities discussed in this chapter—empathy, curiosity, and humility—which do you find easiest to express? Which do you find the hardest?
- Whom do you know who embodies these three qualities the best?
- How might these three qualities improve your relationships with others? How might they improve communities? the world?

In Luke, Mary is, understandably, very afraid when she encounters the angel Gabriel. Yet through her willingness to fulfill her God-given calling, her fear turns to joy. Magrey deVega writes:

> The opportunity to serve is what pivoted her life from fear to joy. That joy was palpable in Mary's life as she ran to meet her cousin Elizabeth, in what was an amazing scene in Luke 1. These are two people who, by all reasonable expectations, should not be pregnant. But they were.
>
> Mary was too young. Elizabeth was too old.
>
> Mary just got her school ID card. Elizabeth had her AARP card.
>
> Mary wasn't old enough to drive. And Elizabeth probably shouldn't.
>
> Mary still had her whole life ahead of her. Elizabeth couldn't imagine a whole life inside her.
>
> Yet both of them had this one thing in common: God had gotten them involved—involved in a special project

that would improve the lives of others forever beginning with Mary, who would give birth to the Messiah, and Elizabeth, who would give birth to God's messenger.

So when Mary walked into Elizabeth's house, all heaven broke loose. Elizabeth burst out in loud, joyous screaming. Her baby, John, turned her womb into a bouncy castle. She exclaimed, "God has blessed you above all women, and he has blessed the child you carry" (v. 42).

And Mary responded with some of the most powerful words in the entire Bible, and the most joyful song in the Gospels....

Mary and Elizabeth, the two most central figures in the original Christmas story, were both transformed from fear to joy, after discovering the delight of serving others with love.

Consider these reflection questions from the author:

- When has fear ever blocked your sense of joy?
- When have you experienced the joy of giving yourself in generosity to others?
- What is God calling you to do, to move you from fear to joy by serving others?

CLOSING ACTIVITY AND PRAYER

Unwrap the appropriate box from the centerpiece and put the item symbolizing joy on display.

Read the Magnificat out loud, verse by verse, allowing different participants to read the verses as desired:

"With all my heart I glorify the Lord!
In the depths of who I am I rejoice in God my savior.

He has looked with favor on the low status of his servant.
    Look! From now on, everyone will consider me highly favored
        because the mighty one has done great things for me.
Holy is his name.
    He shows mercy to everyone,
        from one generation to the next,
        who honors him as God.
He has shown strength with his arm.
    He has scattered those with arrogant thoughts and proud inclinations.
    He has pulled the powerful down from their thrones
        and lifted up the lowly.
He has filled the hungry with good things
    and sent the rich away empty-handed.
He has come to the aid of his servant Israel,
    remembering his mercy,
    just as he promised to our ancestors,
        to Abraham and to Abraham's descendants forever."

                                              (Luke 1:46-55)

Closing Prayer

Lord, God of Mary, Father of Jesus, you lift up the lowly and you scatter the proud. Let us, like Mary, be filled with joy as we bear your spirit into the world. Amen.

SESSION 4

FULLY DIVINE

Peace through Christ

(Colossians 1:15-20)

SESSION 4

FULLY DIVINE

Peace through Christ

(Colossians 1:15-20)

This chapter focuses on the theme of peace, with the encouragement that the story of Christ's existence expands our conception of peace. Breaking the power of sin and death, Christ's life does far more than invite passive participation in the absence of conflict. Jesus Christ's shattering of the dominions of darkness invites us to join in the creation of a just world moving toward God's kingdom. Christ's birth ushers believers into a light that leads to perfect peace. As the journey of *The Christmas Letters* draws to an end, the author invites readers to reflect on how they will integrate their lives with the Christmas story going forward.

As the book sessions end, it's a great opportunity for you to reflect on your experience as a leader. What have you learned from leading this study? Would you do it again? What would you change? How has the study deepened your own faith? How will this study affect your Christmas season this year?

Planning the Session

Session Goals

By the end of this session, participants will be able to:

- explain what the peace of Christ means in the context of the Scriptures,
- apply the concept of the peace of Christ to their own context, and
- sum up learnings from the entire study.

Preparation

- Gather materials needed
  - ◊ Advent wreath with candles
  - ◊ Matches or lighter
  - ◊ Candles for participants that can easily be held
  - ◊ Wrapped gifts centerpiece (see Preparation in session 1)
- Read through the chapter and leader guide, and watch the video.
- Pray for the session and its participants.

Opening Activity and Prayer

Open your session by reading aloud this quotation from chapter 4 of *The Christmas Letters*:

> Because all things are in Christ, and because Christ is in all things, and because we are part of the creation that Christ has both created and drawn into himself, we are part of God's greatest work in history: reconciliation.
>
> Another word for that is *peace*, which is our final key word for Advent.

Because of the Incarnation, Crucifixion, and resurrection of Jesus, there is one thing that is even more infinite than the stars of the universe and the atoms in your body. It is the capacity and power of love that pulls us together, so that we can forge relationships of peace with one another and all of creation.

Invite participants to name areas of their lives in which they experience peace.

Light the Advent candles of hope, joy, peace, and love.

Opening Prayer

God of peace, bring our hearts together as one during this time. Prepare us to receive this time with open hands and hearts, as we anticipate meeting the Christ Child. Expand our knowledge of the divinity and humanity of Christ, and how our lives are wrapped up in his. Amen.

WATCH THE VIDEO

Play session 4: "Fully Divine: Peace through Christ" on *The Christmas Letters* DVD or via Amplify Media.

Discuss:

- Did anything specific stand out as you watched the video?
- How does Magrey deVega describe the relationship between the human and divine aspects of Jesus?
- How does the incarnation of Christ point to peace in our world? Peace for us as individuals?
- What is something you learned that you didn't know before?

Invite the group to keep both the video and the book in mind throughout the discussion below.

STUDY AND DISCUSSION

In chapter 4 of *The Christmas Letters*, Magrey deVega bases his discussion on Colossians 1:15-20. Take the time to read through this passage as a group, with different readers taking different verses.

After you have read through the passage once, use the questions below to explore the Scripture passage in depth. Questions are listed after the verses.

> ^{15} The Son is the image of the invisible God,
>   the one who is first over all creation,
>
> ^{16} Because all things were created by him:
>   both in the heavens and on the earth,
>   the things that are visible and the things that are invisible.
>   Whether they are thrones or powers,
>   or rulers or authorities,
>   all things were created through him and for him.

- What does it mean to you that the Son is the image of God? How do we reconcile this idea with the notion that all humans are created in the image of God?
- Where in the created world do you see evidence of the Son? What in the natural world points you to Jesus?
- What are the thrones, powers, rulers, and authorities mentioned here?
- If thrones, powers, rulers, and authorities were ultimately created through the Son, what does this say about the relationship between earthly power and divine power?
- What hope does it give you to think that all things, both visible and invisible, ultimately come from God?

¹⁷*He existed before all things,*
   and all things are held together in him.

- What thoughts or images come to mind when you hear the word *eternity*? What about *infinity*?
- What do you think it means that "all things are held together" in Jesus?
- Magrey deVega describes how "Jesus is the only center that can hold." How can you put Christ at the center of your life?

¹⁸*He is the head of the body, the church,*
who is the beginning,
   the one who is firstborn from among the dead
   so that he might occupy the first place in everything.

- Does "the beginning... firstborn from among the dead" refer to Christ or to the church?
- What is the relationship between Christ's resurrection and the resurrection hope that we hold as Jesus's followers?
- How can the church hold up the hope of resurrection for the whole world?

¹⁹*Because all the fullness of God was pleased to live in him,*
   ²⁰*and he reconciled all things to himself through him—*
   whether things on earth or in the heavens.
      He brought peace through the blood of his cross.

- How do verses 15-17 help us interpret the phrase "all the fullness of God?"
- How does God's dwelling in Jesus bring about reconciliation of all things?
- What is the relationship between peace and reconciliation?

- How does "the blood of his cross" bring about peace? What new significance do you find in Jesus's death based on the whole of Colossians 1:15-20?
- In the Pauline Epistles, sin is often personified as a master that enslaves us. The cross breaks the power of sin and frees us. Have you ever experienced the feeling of being enslaved from sin? Have you ever felt the power of those chains being broken? What was that like for you?

Now, transition to a discussion of the book more specifically.

The author discusses how important songs were to faith formation, both to the early Christians and in our lives today. He mentions especially the "reminiscence bump," in which we can most easily remember songs from our late adolescence/early young adulthood. Magrey deVega writes,

> It is during that formative period of our lives when our identity and personhood most take shape. So the music we listen to as teens and young adults bears an intrinsic link to critical and memorable events in our personal development: the significant choices we were making, the long-term relationships we were forming, the first glimpses of independence we were experiencing, and the cultural, political, and religious beliefs we were choosing to view the world.
>
> So the reminiscence bump phenomena suggest that when you listen to that music now, you can not only remember the lyrics, you can remember who you were and who you are.

These songs are not just musical icons, but also transform us spiritually.

Fully Divine

- What songs constitute your "reminiscence bump"? When you hear these songs, what do you recall about your younger self?
- What songs come to mind when you think about the adolescent stage of your faith? Were there hymns or songs that you associate with the early days of your belief?
- In what ways has your life been transformed by Jesus, like the characters in the Christmas narrative?

In Colossians 1, the apostle uses an early Christian hymn to communicate the meaning of Christ's incarnation—a song that he hoped would become formative for the early church.

The Christ hymn of Colossians centers the power and mystery of God revealed in Christ, linking our humanity to God's divinity. The author invites us to use these hymns to reflect on our own faith.

- When you consider Jesus, what do you come to know about God?
- How does pondering the infinity and vastness of the universe expand your view of Jesus?
- How will you make Jesus the center of your life?

Reflecting on the entire journey of reading and reflecting on *The Christmas Letters*, the author invites us to sum up the time of studying and growing. Magrey deVega writes,

> Romans showed us the beauty of the long view, both as a remembrance of the past and the work of God into the future. Just as the birth of Jesus was part of a grand story that stretched from the beginning of time and into eternity, God is working in your life the same way. Remember what God has done in your life, and give thanks. Claim the promised future that God is unfolding in your life, and don't give up.

The epistles of John help us to see the incarnation of Jesus as a fulfillment of God's intended creation (Genesis), a light for us amid the darkness (the Gospel of John), and an embodiment of God's love for all people (1 John). Whenever you are feeling lost and confused, Jesus is there for you through the fellowship of others, as you surround one another in relationships of both love and truth.

Philippians points us to the way of Jesus, who embodied humility, curiosity, and empathy. These are important antidotes to the brokenness and division that plague our culture today. By becoming fully human, and obedient to the mission to which God had called him, he showed us how to offer ourselves in service to others. The Incarnation therefore gives us a pathway to both servanthood and joy, as we fully live into our potential and make a difference in the world.

And here, in Colossians, we see the incarnation of Christ's glorious divinity. He was there since the beginning, as Creator of all things. He lives in us still, cocreating a new future for each of us who calls him Lord. As we ponder the wonder of the infant Jesus, we see in his face the glory of all that has been created, and we even discover the potential of new creation within ourselves. We see in Jesus all that has been, will be, and is becoming, moment by moment.

The crucial question for us is, what difference will this make in our lives? Discuss the following questions:

- How will you make the Christmas story more than something you remember, but instead something you live out?

Fully Divine

- What will you do to make sure you don't miss what God wants to reveal to you this Christmas?
- What key insights have you learned from this Advent journey? How will you apply them all year round?

CLOSING ACTIVITY AND PRAYER

Unwrap the appropriate box from the centerpiece and put the item symbolizing joy on display.

Allow time for each participant to name an area of their lives, communities, or the world in which peace is needed.

Each participant is invited to light a candle for peace, while holding in contemplation the situations in need of peace named above.

Closing Prayer

Pray the prayer of Saint Francis with candles lit:

Lord, make me an instrument of your peace:
where there is hatred, let me sow love;
where there is injury, pardon;
where there is doubt, faith;
where there is despair, hope;
where there is darkness, light;
where there is sadness, joy.
O divine Master, grant that I may not so much seek
to be consoled as to console,
to be understood as to understand,
to be loved as to love.
For it is in giving that we receive,
it is in pardoning that we are pardoned,
and it is in dying that we are born to eternal life.
Amen.

WATCH VIDEOS BASED ON THE CHRISTMAS LETTERS: CELEBRATING ADVENT WITH THOSE WHO TOLD THE STORY FIRST WITH MAGREY R. DEVEGA THROUGH AMPLIFY MEDIA.

Amplify Media is a multimedia platform that delivers high-quality, searchable content with an emphasis on Wesleyan perspectives for churchwide, group, or individual use on any device at any time. In a world of sometimes overwhelming choices, Amplify gives church leaders and congregants media capabilities that are contemporary, relevant, effective and, most important, affordable and sustainable.

With *Amplify Media* church leaders can:

- Provide a reliable source of Christian content through a Wesleyan lens for teaching, training, and inspiration in a customizable library
- Deliver their own preaching and worship content in a way the congregation knows and appreciates
- Build the church's capacity to innovate with engaging content and accessible technology
- Equip the congregation to better understand the Bible and its application
- Deepen discipleship beyond the church walls

Ask your group leader or pastor about Amplify Media
and sign up today at www.AmplifyMedia.com.

www.ingramcontent.com/pod-product-compliance
Lightning Source LLC
Chambersburg PA
CBHW011344090426
42743CB00019B/3435